W9-AFV-722

To Evelyn - C.R.

First published in the United States of America in 1997
by Walker Publishing Company, Inc.

Until I Met Dudley copyright © Frances Lincoln Ltd. 1997
Fiction text copyright © Roger McGough 1997
Nonfiction text compiled by Moira Butterfield and Douglas Maxwell
copyright © Frances Lincoln Limited 1997
Illustrations copyright © Chris Riddell 1997

Until I Met Dudley was edited, designed, and produced by Frances Lincoln Ltd.
4 Torriano Mews, Torriano Avenue, London NW5 2RZ

All rights reserved. No part of this book may be reproduced or transmitted in any form
or by any means, electronic or mechanical, including photocopying, recording, or by
any information storage and retrieval system, without permission in writing from the Publisher.

All the characters and events portrayed in this work are fictitious.

Library of Congress Cataloging-in-Publication Data
McGough, Roger.
Until I met Dudley: how everyday things really work / Roger McGough;
illustrations by Chris Riddell.
p.   cm.
Summary : A young girl used to have fantastic ideas about how things work,
but Dudley tells her how it really is. Explains the workings of mechanical objects such
as vacuum cleaners, refrigerators, dishwashers, toasters, and garbage trucks.
ISBN 0-8027-8623-5 (hardcover).—ISBN 0-8027-8624-3 (reinforced)
1. Household appliances, Electric—Juvenile literature.
[1. Technology.] I. Riddell, Chris, ill. II. Title.
TK7019.M33 1997
683'.8—dc21   96-47900
                                                                                          CIP
                                                                                          AC

Printed in Hong Kong
2 4 6 8 10 9 7 5 3 1

Until I Met Dudley

How everyday things really work

ROGER M^cGOUGH

Illustrations by **CHRIS RIDDELL**

WALKER AND COMPANY

NEW YORK

When you put the slices of bread into the toaster and push the handle down, an alarm goes off underground, telling the toast elves to spring into action.
A friendly dragon toasts the bread with his fiery breath (but sometimes he breathes too hard!). Cogwheels and conveyor belts, treadmills and telescopes — it's all so simple!

until I met Dudley . . .

Dudley showed me how a toaster works . . .

1. A toaster needs electricity to work, so check to see that it's plugged in. Pop a slice of bread (or two if you're hungry!) into one of the slots in the top. The bread sits inside the toaster on a **bread rack** that is attached to a **spring**.

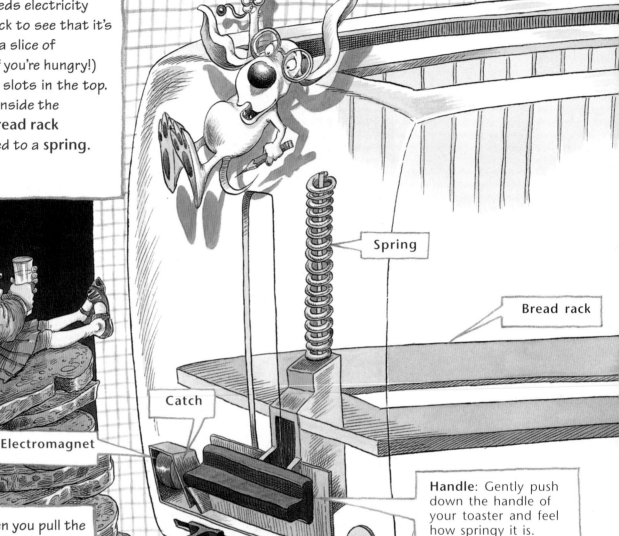

Spring

Bread rack

Catch

Electromagnet

Handle: Gently push down the handle of your toaster and feel how springy it is.

2. *ZZZZPP!* When you pull the toaster handle down, the spring s-t-r-e-t-c-h-e-s and the bread rack moves down. *CLICK!* The rack is now locked in place with a small **catch**.

Browning control: Use this to choose how dark you want your toast.

3. Electricity zooms along tiny wires called **heating elements** on either side of the bread rack. They become so hot that they start to glow, heating the soft bread and turning it into crunchy toast.

4. When the elements heat up, so does a little strip made of two different metals. This strip is called a **bimetallic strip**. When it gets hot, one of the metals grows larger than the other. This makes the strip bend and touch the **tripping plate**.

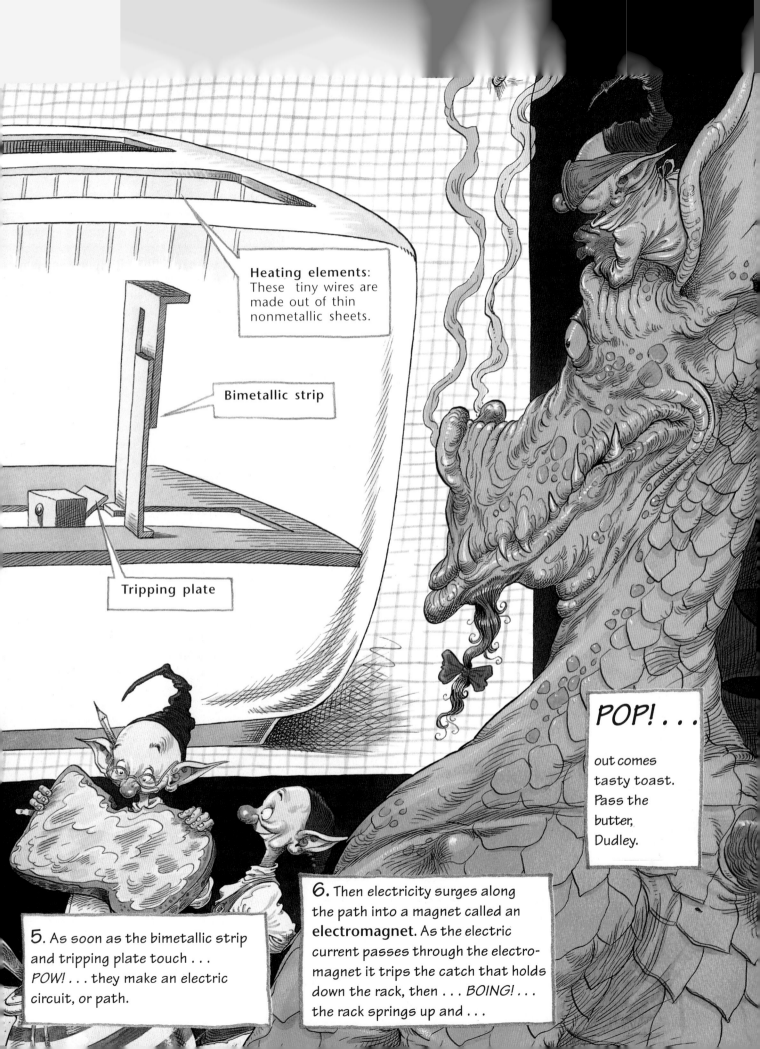

Heating elements: These tiny wires are made out of thin nonmetallic sheets.

Bimetallic strip

Tripping plate

POP! . . .

out comes tasty toast. Pass the butter, Dudley.

5. As soon as the bimetallic strip and tripping plate touch . . . POW! . . . they make an electric circuit, or path.

6. Then electricity surges along the path into a magnet called an **electromagnet**. As the electric current passes through the electromagnet it trips the catch that holds down the rack, then . . . BOING! . . . the rack springs up and . . .

You load the dishwasher, put in the detergent, then turn it on. The switch is linked to a special siren that makes a high-pitched whistle that can be heard only by cats.

At the signal, all the cats in the neighborhood come running to your house and climb into the machine through a special cat-flap at the back. (That's the banging you hear.) They lick all the plates, cups, pans, and utensils clean, singing happily to themselves. (That's the humming you hear.)

When everything is nice and clean, they leave, the last one out sprinkling the detergent around the machine to get rid of any cat smells.

until I met Dudley . . .

Dudley showed me how a dishwasher works . . .

1. Before pressing the start button, always fill the dishwasher **dispensers** with a cleaner called **dishwasher detergent** and a liquid called **rinse-aid**. Together, they help the dishwasher to wash away glop and make the dishes sparkly clean.

2. Once the machine is loaded and switched on, it controls the whole washing process by working through a step-by-step program. *CLICK* . . . step one: Cold water gushes into the bottom of the machine through a small **inlet pipe**.

3. *CLICK* . . . step two: An electric pump pushes the water out through the **spray arms**. These are like garden sprinklers. They whiz around very fast, spraying water over the dishes and getting rid of those blobs of ketchup *(UGH!)*, leftover bits of brussels sprouts *(YUK!)*, and other food.

Outlet pipe: Dirty, smelly water escapes through here.

Inlet pipe: Clean water swooshes in through a valve that opens and shuts like a gate.

Filter: Water drains through here.

4. Next, the dirty water drains down through a hole covered with a **filter**. This works like a fishing net, catching all the bits of food that have been washed off the dishes. Remember to clean the filter from time to time, removing any food that is still there.

Spray arms: Water sprays out through tiny holes.

Dish rack

5. So what happens to all that dirty water? It disappears through another pipe called an **outlet pipe** . . . *GURGLE, GURGLE* . . . and eventually into the drain outside. *CLICK!* Clean water rushes into the bottom of the machine. This mixes with the detergent, heats up, and sprays out of the whizzing spray arms to clean the dishes.

Detergent dispenser

Rinse-aid dispenser

6. Finally . . . *WHOOSH!* Cold water pours in again and mixes with the rinse-aid liquid to rinse the detergent off the dishes. The mixture heats up, sprays out, and then drains away through the outlet pipe, leaving the dishes to dry.

Program dial: Use this to choose and control the dishwashing steps.

Special polar bears arrive every night to deliver blocks of ice cut from icebergs floating in the oceans of the Arctic. They pack the refrigerator with the ice and make sure everything is cold enough before leaving.

   As the ice begins to melt, water runs down the back of the fridge into a secret compartment at the bottom. Here, it flows into a waterwheel, which drives a fan that spins cool air to keep the fridge cold.

until I met Dudley . . .

Dudley showed me how a refrigerator works . . .

1. The refrigerator is a big box that keeps food cold so that it stays fresh longer. It uses a mystery ingredient called a **refrigerant**, which runs through hidden pipes in the walls of the fridge.

2. On its journey around the maze of pipes, the refrigerant removes heat from the inside of the fridge, keeping it cool. It does this by changing back and forth from a runny liquid to an invisible gas.

3. The refrigerant begins its journey as a gas. It is then compressed by an electric pump called a **compressor**. The compressor squeezes the gas into a small space where it starts to turn into a liquid because of all the pressure.

4. This changing of gas to liquid gives off heat as it is pumped through a long snakelike tube called a **condenser** on the outside at the back of the refrigerator. Heat passes through the tube into the open air like heat coming out of a radiator. That's why the back of the refrigerator feels hot.

5. Then, as the cold liquid flows into a wider tube in the **evaporator**, the pressure relaxes and presto! . . . the liquid turns back into a gas.

Evaporator: Here the liquid turns to gas and absorbs heat.

Condenser: Heat passes through this into the open air.

Compressor: This works like a heart, pumping the refrigerant around the refrigerator.

Dust is the favorite food of the vacuum snake.
He sleeps curled up inside the tube until the
vacuum cleaner is switched on. He has a huge
appetite and is a noisy eater, gobbling up
all the dust, crumbs, and buttons he can find.

When a vacuum snake is full, he waits until midnight then slithers outside and sneezes! The trouble is, he always leaves the door wide open so that the wind blows the dust back in.

until I met Dudley . . .

Dudley showed me how a vacuum cleaner works . . .

1. A vacuum cleaner is powered by a small **motor** that runs on electricity. So, before switching it on, it needs to be plugged in to a nearby socket.

2. *WHIRRRR!* Once the motor is running, it turns a **fan** around and around. As the fan spins, it pushes air out of the vacuum cleaner through a tube called a **duct**.

3. Because air is pushed *out* of the vacuum cleaner, even more air gets sucked *in* to take its place, just like water being sucked up through a straw.

4. And as air gets sucked up through the **hose**, so does dirt and dust.

5. *SSLLUUUUP!* All this dust is then sucked into a **dust bag**. But where does the air go? It escapes through tiny holes in the walls of the bag. The dirt and dust are trapped inside; they're too big to get through the holes.

6. The dust bag fills up and after a while needs emptying or replacing. If you don't keep an eye on it, it becomes so full that it . . .

Hose

Duct

Electric motor

Fan

Head: This is attached to the hose. Air gets sucked in here.

Dust bag

This is an upright vacuum cleaner. Instead of a hose, it has a **roller** with tiny, stiff **brushes** sticking out of it. It spins the brushes around and around, beating the carpet. This stirs up the dust, which is sucked into the cleaner.

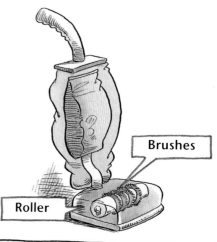

Brushes

Roller

BURSTS!

I thought I knew how a garbage truck worked . . .

Pigs are kept inside the truck. The garbage
is emptied into troughs at the back where
the pigs stuff themselves. They're the happiest
pigs in the world!

until I met Dudley . . .

Dudley showed me how a garbage truck works . . .

Warning light

1. A garbage truck is a big can on wheels, usually operated by a team of two or more people. The driver sits in the cab. He keeps the engine running to provide the power for the garbage truck to do its job.

2. The other sanitation workers on the team pick up garbage cans and lift them onto a **platform** at the back of the truck . . . *CLONK, CLINK, CLUNK.* **Clamps** hold the cans firmly so they can't fall off.

3. The platform, powered by the truck's engine, swings up . . . *WHIRRRR* . . . and tips the garbage out of the cans, into the truck. Then the platform swings down so the sanitation workers can lift off the empty cans and put them back where they belong.

4. Inside the back of the truck there is a wide **scoop** that operates like a huge hand. It's attached to a powerful arm, called a **hydraulic ram.** The ram and scoop work together . . . *CRRUNCH* . . . *SQUUISH* . . . scooping and squashing the trash farther into the truck.

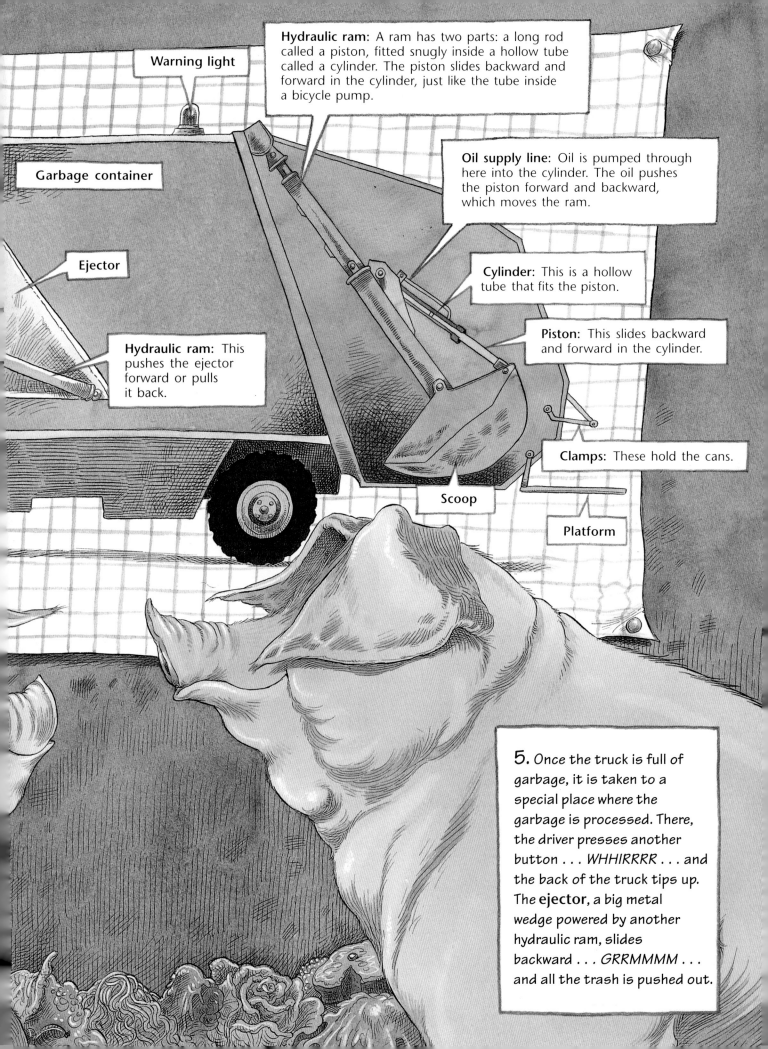

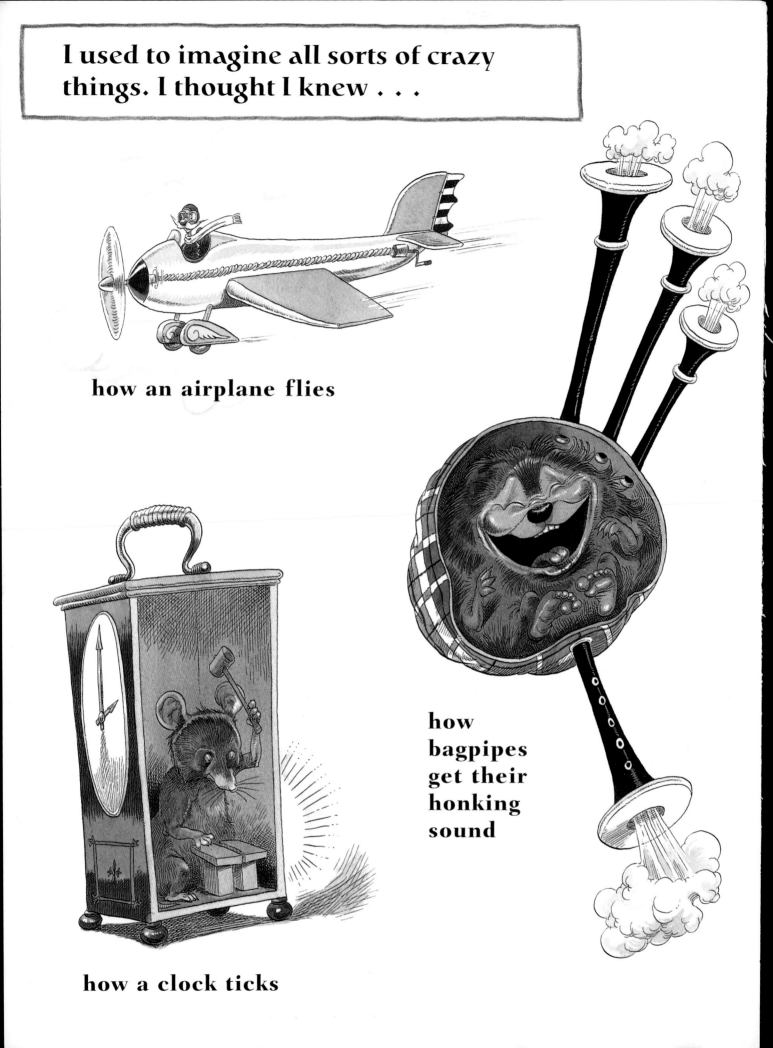

I used to imagine all sorts of crazy things. I thought I knew . . .

how an airplane flies

how bagpipes get their honking sound

how a clock ticks

how large ships keep afloat

how bubbles get into fizzy drinks

how stars
shine at night

. . . until I met Dudley.

I'm really glad I met him.